THE RESTORERS

Phoenix Poets

A SERIES EDITED BY ROBERT VON HALLBERG

W . S . DI PIERO

The Restorers

THE UNIVERSITY OF CHICAGO PRESS

Chicago and London

W. S. Di Piero's other books of poetry are The First Hour, The Only
Dangerous Thing, Early Light, and The Dog Star. He has also published
two books of essays (Memory and Enthusiasm and Out of Eden) and has
translated three books from the Italian (Pensieri, by Giacomo Leopardi;
This Strange Joy: Selected Poems of Sandro Penna; and The Ellipse:
Selected Poems of Leonardo Sinisgalli).

The University of Chicago Press, Chicago 60637
The University of Chicago Press, Ltd., London
© 1992 by The University of Chicago
All rights reserved. Published 1992
Printed in the United States of America

01 00 99 98 97 96 95 94 93 92   5 4 3 2 1

ISBN (cloth): 0-226-15346-0
ISBN (paper): 0-226-15347-9

Library of Congress Cataloging-in-Publication Data

Di Piero, W. S.
      The restorers / W. S. Di Piero.
          p.   cm. — (Phoenix poets)
      I. Title.   II. Series.
      PS3554.I65R47   1992
      811'.54—dc20   91-29065
                        CIP

Contents

Acknowledgments

Grateful acknowledgments are made to the following magazines in which some of the poems in this volume first appeared:

Ironwood: "Two American Speeches"
The New Criterion: "The Two Old Ladies of September," "The Hermit Thrush," "Poem ('Heartsick, settled for good')"
Pequod: "The Hotel Room Mirror," "The Restorers," "The Speech in the Middle of the Night," "Emmaus, "The Museum of Natural History"
Provincetown Arts: "Old Gold"
St. Andrews Review: "Saint Francis of Assisi"
Southern Review: "Poem ('The grass bundle the girl')," "Augustine on the Beach," "The Early Part of the Day"
Southwest Review: "An Unwritten Letter to My Daughter"
The Threepenny Review: "The Faery Child," "Dreaming the Pacific," "Starlings," "After the Sacrifice"
TriQuarterly: "The Caverns," "In Calabria," "The Next Room," "Near Damascus," "Gethsemane," "Poem ('A few bedroom lights')"
ZYZZYVA: "Frankie's Birthday Party"

The author also wishes to thank the John Simon Guggenheim Foundation for its generous support.

one

The Early Part of the Day

Most of them lean into the windless sun,
stretching their necks a little, like birds,
working to keep in motion, at least that.
They take their daily exercise walking the street
down from the rehab center, past my house,
unrighteous, ignoring the sluice of cars,
schoolkids on bikes, buses heaving people
from the cinder-block slum two blocks beyond the center
to gardens, pools, and kitchens one suburb away.
Not quite that far is the new neighborhood park
where the vets, all mental cases, take themselves
before they have to loop back home, a few
dressed out of sync—porkpie hats, bellbottoms—
but with fanatical composure, or disarray
as if they whipped themselves with clothes that stuck.
Their mild faces sit apart, in twos and threes,
and watch the young shining wives cheer their children
down the slide and breeze them high on swings.
The homeless, too, love the park, the sunshine,
thick grass, shade if they need it, the safety
of hidden money those wives and children own.
The blacks and Mexicans who ride the bus

don't stop here. The others, sleeping on the grass,
hug swollen plastic sacks. The morning I saw one
clawing a spill of socks, jars, and paper towels,
I recalled the man, a computer engineer,
who stewed in Dickens and ancient history
to keep him thinking, he told me, after he was lost
for years "in Uncle Sam's premier nuthouse,"
because after the mine went off, his hearing gone,
he's on his knees scooping together his best friend.
I've never noticed here the one young vet
I'd recognize, I've seen him stalk by so often,
the one whose moral sense I slur with this.
He's out of life, or nearly. In his studious, locked,
unmigratory look, as if scrutinizing
each clear zone of air he has to pass through,
knowing he may never pass that way again,
there's Caravaggio's Thomas, squinty, curious,
humming a little, prying open the moist lips
in his Redeemer's side, puzzling out the fact,
inquisitor of a body divine who hopes to find,
in the meat of flesh he's touched, a holiness
they've said will bear him to another life.

The Faery Child

Saying his prayers, he hears them scrape their flesh
up from under the bed, their voices solid, animal,
like those his own chimes with all day, the human ones.

Except for the differentness, like fluted air,
wind through tall bending trees, or owl's cry too drawn out.
Their bodies are their voices. They tell him how to live,

that he will soon return with them, to be of them.
Some days they rise behind the sofa. Giggling, snorting,
they finger the piano and tap the T.V. buttons.

You're not of these things, they say, you can't belong
to this, you belong to the voices of our flesh,
our life's yours, we can make you really glad.

Once, swarming through the door screen from the patio,
hurried in their always near breathing voices,
they closed around him, holding hands, locking dark

on darker air, and he knew he could die for them
and live his heart away, at last, from their sounds
that are so beautiful they rip him from his place,

for they won't let the plain, vaporous, half-seen world
exist for him, their presences like pollen dust
on the keys, the screen-door latch, his books, his pens.

First time he saw them, from the school window, they were
graygreen scarves, tangled in a bush, that turned
to children grown moment to moment into adults,

and now their voices come like scarves to swaddle him,
untouching, cottony, ravishing him away
from engulfment in some middle, necessary world.

The Museum of Natural History

Dawn rises where the great hall ends.
The water hole's twilight shocking pink
erodes to backstage noises, shapes . . .
The antelope's indifferent head
points its antlers toward a wasp nest's
corrugated skull-heap. The sound track
whines and mixes the varieties
of mud's coppery morning song.

And killing ground. The numbed roar
of big cats in the distance cuts through
the other hunger music. Above,
a hooter ridicules creation:
the thirsty me-monkey, the person
snickering nervous in the tree,
waiting to shimmy down and drink
from the clear pool, the source, the ditch.

The diorama's temper fades
toward dusk. We move, outrunning
that shriveled time, into the room
where we feel at once all sorts of blood
laboring separate in our veins,
from savanna's matinal light
to stinking rock moss and pit slime.
The crocodile's muddy blood

pumped twice, a hundred years each time,
whipped the dragon tail to kill
some absent or remembered threat.
Behind, the tortoise was another
blear-veined rock. You turned, stooped,
bent your nose against the glass,
inches from the rattler's head
slung midair from its squat black perch.

I remembered later how you rapped hard,
impatient, at the glass. To startle
or wake the killer's attention?
At lakeside, the blood-drop pricked from rock
was a ladybug's carapace,
flown in a blister of wingbeats
when you drummed your stubby fingertips,
when you drummed your thick red nails.

Adam's Garden

Walking home, I saw them
matched up near the tree,
my shy, mud-faced drudge,
my anxious golden boy,
and could have yelled both back
when I saw his raised hand
swollen through the club,
his fist an oak knob, flesh
gone to green wood,
the whole tree shrieking outraged
offering. That's all.
Blood-puddles at its roots,
under a clear sky,
the tree's still growing.

It's like the blazing stalk
the Angel held, at the rent
in the moist green wall,
pointing out our new work.
Diggers, dung-gatherers,
root-eaters—what else?

He says things could be worse.
He says he kills my son.
He and I know our place,
workpit, dirt, so lovely
when moonlight's littered, gashed,
white ashes everywhere,
God's boneyard we tend
not far from the other gate.

2.

Their green frantic home, the landscape
snarled, memory's jag, flames,
no God there to comb out vines
and thorn-hocks, the God-kissed tree where
my lovely son keeps on dying
in my half-sleep. Roaring, confused,
his softer flesh foams beneath
the other's fist. Then he's a pool.
In it the other's knobby image
rages down, but glassier,
wrinkled, scummed by shadow-spots.
And the pool's a slit, a sinkhole
swallowing both in one silence,
the whole picture glazed over
with rain, vomit trails, gristle
pulped and spread fine upon things.

The more the other one shuts up
and sickens himself with work, the more
the hoarse teenage voice calls to me
near the old wall, whose barbed spines
increase day to day like grass,

but thicker, bunched like weeds or dung-clots,
where the firestalk's scorchmark
still blisters, crackling . . . He speaks
to me from inside, his soft mouth now
green brambles dripping black sap
into my sleep. They dream me.
They're sounds I know I've heard before.
Garbled too deep in the wall, his words
rasp gentle messages whose tone,
unholy and indifferent,
won't tell me what to do.

The Murphy Bed

Our childhood's favorite gag.
A serene drunk tons-o'-fun
in puckered courtly pajamas,
snapped up by the bottom jaw.
All gone. Silence.
The room's larger than before.

How complete, shut up
inside a wall for good.
We knew it had to happen
sooner or later to us.

The film jerked and ran.
The man slammed down,
delivered, but that
was wasted joy on us.

Now instead of that story
I see a woman there,
her hair black and frizzed,
a small mole on her shoulder.
A blouse on the carpet,
shoes and pantyhose in a heap.

Her man steps close, checks
the bedside clock, then sees her
grab the burst of hair
and push it high on her head.

Still not touching her,
he falls back on the sheet,
breathing softly, waiting,
while we stay as we are.

Starlings

Snarls, bread trucks, yeast
breathing inside huddled bags,
and sleepers completing lives
behind their gray windows.

A whistle on the phonewires,
feathers, twitches, whistling
down to the hot loaves.

Reeds everywhere, pulse,
flesh, flutes, and wakened sighs.
An answer. Radio news

and breathers behind our windows,
birds' new voices changing,
changed, to the unforgiving
hunger screech of immigrants.

Poem

Your bleared features behind the scuffed plastic oval
cringe with rain
that scores image
and headstone, sluicing channels underground.
A mild look that seems to want other knowledge,
the fair oblivion of the ditch,
of hair, ash, and bone.
In your half-smile, half-knowledge the photographer found
in dusty studio light:
stars' distance, starlight's nearness,
your fingers touching a man's hair,
your kiss on a child's forehead,
your throat and breast flaming
when someone noticed you.

This votive token, saving that,
gives up everything else.
The heavenward mind,
seeing gods and goats in starlines,
rots in the ground.

Where's deity in mud and metals?
Heads in the clouds, we live underworld, boneless shades,
imagining ourselves real and real again.
Staring off to one side,
desirous, bemused,
for you existence was liturgy,
the god-wish in your look, your gestures,
your skull and dust.
Rainwater cuts that presence, following you down.

(After Giacomo Leopardi's *Sopra il ritratto di una
bella donna*)

Emmaus

The way he offered things
was first to take them from you.
You can (he seemed to say)
possess all life, but give me
all you will ever want.

The knife, the cup, the bread,
he grabbed them without a word,
to house the sense we had
of miraculous contagion.
His goodwill hissed like rage.

And then I thought he spoke.
But that was heat pulsing
from nerveless, mudgray flesh,
and a humming all around him
that I've felt in lightning storms.

We met his affronted silence
with an empire's keen, belched noise,
the humble oohs and grunts
that mocked his outraged offer
to burn old lives away.

Holding out the bread,
he pointed at my ripped sleeve,
and his curt thanks for bounty,
his first words, were laid
along the knife's tough blade.

To eat of bread he touched,
to taste those angry words,
changed the feel of time.
That's how I knew, at last,
he had come back for us

whose anger measures love.
When he left—where he was,
he wasn't—we too gave thanks
for the heat-sick wind and rain
drummed up in his absence.

We argued half the night,
drunk with explanations.
We'd known whose god he was.
Now we knew what kind. For love,
we ate our own green want.

Two American Speeches

1.

"**M**oney is really good shit,
nordamericano stuff,
greenbacks, but for shit
you need decent plumbing,
you need banks. Bananas,
copper, coffee, zinc.

"We like our Christ bloodied,
gashed and shot up,
flayed, balls stuffed
in his bruised mouth.
Pilate's a Botero clown
sporting a lacquer moustache,

"a solemn porky greaser
that grows like wild
in our heat and rain
south of your concern.
Sprouting like our strange fruit,
like our fat happy poor."

2.

"I wanted to say Mass, but the others
said we still had too far to go.
Just then, they looked like the Elect,
rag bundles sagging on their backs,
like the rough shirts the women sewed
from dozens of boiled scraps.
With the river flowing there,
the frontier, whose flowing in the sun
I thought was like Christ's blood.
The birds really do bear messages.
Strange how they all came,
thousands, and so quickly,
because we wanted another place.
The peasants in their white shirts
wanted land. But mainly,
they wanted to be left alone.
We thought we'd stop and pray
beyond the river. We thought,
when the soldiers showed up,
they would take us back.
That was all right, I knew
I could always say Mass later.
But after they left,
after they shot everyone
and cut up many and put the pieces
into the river, the vultures came
to make it like a black carpet.
I thought, Would Christ our Lord
walk upon that water?
And waddle like Charlot
about to lose his blissful balance?"

The Next Room

Like leaves and coils of leaf dust
turning along the sidewalk

beyond my view; like wind
picking the flared leaf mounds

at the curb . . . It's all
and nothing like. Something else:

a cool sweep of air I felt
the moment you walked in

and jabbed the radio,
squealing across the band

(the way you draw speech from
the cockeyed cabinet hinge)

unseen, one room away,
but for the brazen sun-sleeve

cast across my rug
from the door you meant to close.

Careening, famished, cupboard
to fridge, you reach me here

in a thinned-out shadow
crossing the bar of light,

lapping it, like the subway's
blued radiance that raked

the scummy street grates; machine-
oiled draft razzed up

through the reef. Deeper,
small change cringed in the muck,

waiting to be claimed. ("Well,
they're lost for good!") The shadow

passes. It's the smell
of leaves blown through the door,

it's the chair leg scraping the floor
when you climb up and reach.

Anna at Eighteen

Diamond-chip earrings for Mass,
a plastic garment bag, or shoe rack,
an ottoman fan, a toaster—
the broken stacks of Raleigh coupons
streaking across the table.
Maybe a ceramic lighter
to replace her war surplus Zippo,
the first morning smoke
brushing the crimped piles
while her mother counted coupons
nearly every day, like leaves
from no tree on their street;
the one sycamore's dusty things
scummed the ground during fall rains.
Wedged among the stacks, the daily crossword,
solutions tooled, ballpoint ghosts
spidering up and down the news
four pages deep: I K E   H I F I
that meant no more to her than E S S O
but called to her and made her lost
like the day she crouched in the dugout
exit of the nigger church, the live butt

someone had tossed to the curb
pinched between her fingers;
bums slept and left their smell down there,
but there were wild hymns on Sunday nights,
and handclapped prayer, piano pounding,
and the butcher-shop smell of absolution
when her hand smoked under the ember
kissing her palm. Auroras,
when she thinks, these mornings,
in her mother's old place . . .
Auroras, too, skating across the sky's
crystal skull, flow with the juice
of stars and planets, like autumn rain
falling across the phonelines,
the red brickface and windows,
the universe's bloodless smear
she saw that day from her school desk;
under the uniform, steam heat
prickled her thighs, the dab of burnt flesh
pulsed in her throat while the sister
whined a spelling list, words blunt
as titles in her picture-study book:
The Gleaners, The Song of the Lark,
The Sower who, when she shuts her eyes,
completes his gesture, tossing the gift
of fire-seeds that sear through the air
and never fall to ground.

Poem

The grass bundle the girl
brings back from the fields
ignites flakes of sundown falling from her shoulders
to the violets and roses in her fist,
Sunday flowers, the kind she'll pin
to her hair, her bodice.
Out front, huddled with her cronies,
somebody's maiden aunt holds the spot
still warmed by late light:
she's unpacking the same old story,
her own lost time when, still lean and quick,
every Sunday she got dressed up
and danced all night with men she knew
in that old perfection.

It's already getting dark,
the sky's famous sober blue comes back;
in moonlight's newest candor shadows hurry down
from the hills and rooftops.
Church bells bang out tomorrow's news—
no work, no work. Hearing that,
we'd say the news, for once, sounds good.

Boys foam into the little piazza,
hopfrogging flagstones, their shrieks
like wind flaying the fieldhand walking by,
shouldering his hoe, headed toward
a meal of lard and lentils,
toward Sunday, when he can pause.

      Then everything's quiet.
The lights go out. That's when we hear
the hammer and saw, the carpenter
pushing all night
to finish a job by the oil lamp
before dawn breaks.
      The best of seven,
today's engorged with wish and joy;
tomorrow's time ripens
dread and sadness—
by then we're already crushed by work
we know we'll have to do.
      But none of that
for you, sunny child;
you can drown in happiness
and breathe the sweet day's season
of existence. If you're lucky,
no Sunday joy
will sicken you too soon.

(After Giacomo Leopardi's *Il sabato del villaggio*)

Augustine on the Beach

The tide quickens. The sun chills down.
The local drifter in his chewed-up hat
shuffles toward the funneled hole:
for days now, a chubby ten-year-old
kneels, digs, dumping buckets of sea
into the pit, back and forth,
surf to beach, smudging prints
left by the nervous sandpipers.
Nothing changes. The hobo, yelling,
flags his hat. They rehearse the script.
The dirigible's dragon shade
absorbs us. The calm boy explains
he's "working the ocean," that soon
he'll finally have it emptied out.
The other, like a wild parent,
shouts not to waste his long life
repeating mysteries of faith.
The big baby fumbles pail and sand.
The man says, has already said
all the days I've been witness here,
to look out there, at those seals
watching us, intent, undesirous,
beyond the agonized sea spray
that shouts for us from the rocks.

The Two Old Ladies
of September

Arm in arm,
they seemed lost,
nudging each other
step and half-step
through the fog,

though cyclamens,
the few poor
sagging blooms
aflame in their fists,
said they've known

these fields for years,
those woods, that pond
where dragonflies
thrummed in bandy
too-tall reeds.

Their drift, a migrant
anger, slantwise,
toward the field
so green, flowers
lush and abundant

last year, before
a long dry spell
cut the soil
a jigsaw scramble
of brown clay.

Their knowledge enraged
by two girls playing
skip-the-crack,
jangling bracelets
strung of red petals,

hooting, waving,
till the ladies
shrieked back: Jump!
Maybe this time the ground
won't eat you for new blood!

Saint Francis of Assisi

The View

The plain's hatching now
after rainless months.

A dust devil rips
through a peach orchard

down there, a seam snuffed
by falling dust-fruit.

Behind the vine rows'
shriveled abundance

a low fire runs
ragged by the ditch,

flaying the pale sod.
The voided skins wave.

September, thirsting,
sings our Hosannah,

shrieks red poverties
to old heaven's eye.

. . . .

1944

You want February? Snow and sleet came down hard,
heaven's post-Christmas gift to freeze our eyelids shut.
Walking the icy ground, our shoes all shot with holes,
we did the Alexander's Army Ragtime Dance,
stomping snow off bones safely packed in newspapers.
From down below, we must have looked crazy happy,
dancing like Hollywood Indians, though who had
anything to eat? We dreamed lard. So the wolves came,
not straight into town, not into the piazza,
but near the outcrop behind the church. God's design,
the best, the way they study the tired world
makes them next to human, or more. They're waiting
while they move. I'd worship that expectancy.
If I could talk to one, just a few minutes,
he'd teach me hunger's secrets. So one awful night
I wrapped my legs and feet, stuffed more papers inside
my pants and shirt, then danced my way behind the church.
Faint gray writing on the snow. Skin and bones, sneezes,
frost feathers, drifting away. Two of them walked back,
canny bigshot archbishop warrior types. They said:
The moon's blue, we know you want secrets, help, advice,
news from this side. Our truth is: Forget likenesses,
live inside your carbon soul, the moon's black and blue,
in the soul's time the world's one winter together.

. . . .

Renunciation

The snowy poplar seeds are everywhere,
balling against curbs and car wheels,

sifting through gates, doorways, kitchen windows,
snagged by white blossoms shaken loose

from the nodding horse-chestnut leaves. We stand
in their shadows—our springtime's dark.

The debris scrapes our cheeks, clings an instant
to our lashes, chokes the soft breath

before tumbling off the near precipice.
We want divine uncertainty.

O give us the Judas tree's blood shadows,
make us sick with rank pear blossoms,

blind us with earth's random pieces engorged
with broom's milky fallen-sun flesh.

t w o

The Restorers

(Strozzi Chapel, Santa Maria Novella)

> *S. Philip was taken of the payims, which would*
> *constrain him to make sacrifice to an idol, and anon*
> *under the idol issued out a right, great dragon, and the*
> *dragon corrupted the people with breath that they*
> *were all sick.*

Backlit shades groan through the green nets,
trailing voices along the scaffold's bones.
A sweet roll maybe   *Water!*   *It's too cold*
And coffee, sure   On the next, just-finished wall
the demon, a knotty razorback muscle,
explodes the altar's marble base and coils
at Philip's feet. The saint, looking down,
points at Mars up on his glassy perch
jabbing a snaggled lance at that old heaven,
pilasters braced by 3-D breastplates,
greaves, smashed racking wheels; the god's place
engorged with flags, amphorae, empire's
crabbed junkwares to thicken the inaction.
Courtiers, soldiers, burnt-out believers,
huddle both sides of the altar's
detonated symmetries.

A small Redeemer, smeared top right
in an afterthought of sunshine,
drags his cross back toward sea-voices
crooning behind their mask.   *Look at this*
It's cold enough   Handwork, to reclaim
or fulfill some memory print.   *See?*

Filippino's style already restored
in this image of the high priest's son,
stung by the dragon, dying in a merchant's arms.
A century's discipline of hard outline
sags into quivering drapes and folds,
the suffered exactitudes of flesh
now sketchy wrappers, brocades,
ringlet mops roughed and melting
around identical faces. The wall
weeps carnal stress into mere effects.

At my back, an answering noise.
Whispers quizzing the chilled
vacancy of our atonements.
The three teenage girls, hand in hand,
are Graces dancing a shaggy circle
before Masaccio's *Trinity.*
Their interrogating voices slash
the mystery painted into the wall;
dates, technique, influence.
The long, blood-ripened God endures
at one center of one history,
housed, kept, more by imagination
than belief, before voluptuous form
trembled into the nerve ends of style.
The girls genuflect, cross themselves,
stinging the space with energetic facts,

then come this way, hunched and leggy
in their wrinkled coats, clapping florid
gumball-colored gloves, a winter's version
of the image Filippino's teacher made.
They also bring a winter's quiet—
there's less to say of the lesser painter.

No worship, no signs, fewer facts.
They act out a piece of it,
pinch their noses like two figures
in the plaster—only the bulky monster's saved
from nervous drawing. Every word dies
in warm vapors streaming from their lips.
Look here   More water now   They wheeze
laughter through their gloves. Others join us,
aiming cameras at the trembling screen.
Not too much   Not too much this time

We're stuck there, unformed, unfinished,
in time to see the monster driven out.
Less fearful at the latecomer's wall,
the girl whose long, fine-spun curls
brighten the bitter air around her head
talks back to the high secret voices:
"That's hard work, isn't it? And it's
so cold!"   *Not so hard*   "Save it all."
It just takes time   "For us."   *You know?*
"Whatever it is." Someone snaps a picture.
We're still in it, breathing, worlds away
from what Masaccio knew, and turned away
from Philip's scene, too, whose images
our own forms imitate. We're smiling
up toward the floating shades, the voices,
the steady light mashed in the covering web.

The Speech in the Middle of the Night

Out of snarling half-sleep:
Snake hurry and news it good.
Your lips tensed, impassioned
by their nonsense, and fired
the day's cinder facts
like sparks from oil drums.
I thought the dreamy words
would set fire to our room.

Today's front page gave us
that Asian child, boneless,
scorched, in his mother's arms.
Her face looked broken, torn.
He'd die again, you said,
over and over, each time
she'll remember some detail
different yet the same.

· · · · · · · ·

Estranged, unlike, known
but hardly reachable . . .
Remember? You cracked apart
the stony album, bandaged
in browned-out newsprint.

From one scratched plastic slab
you glared back, up, at us.
The snapshot's hellbent wind
fluttered your hair, wrapped it
in redbud branches behind.

Across the black field, worldless,
I glared from another frame
ahead toward us, now,
ghosts from another time,
and the time won't let us breathe.

We forgot, or set aside,
in our hollow of recalled
fond separateness, the mother
and boy, their flesh howling
together, as if we lived alone.

The world belongs to her.
Then to anxious words
needing to hold her knowledge.
We swear on memory:
Desire isn't need.

. . . .

The woman's picture mocked
our album's freight of fact.
Her image, blotting ours,
made you weep. Where is she?
Has she seen the image of herself?
News begs to be forgotten
by newer facts. Against this
we swear not to forget,

even as we want flesh,
and the image of our flesh,
bright shade, preserved without
an image of the world.
When you cried *hurry . . . good!*
the curtains caught some light,
shaken afire by night wind
against the imminent stellar wastes.

Augustine in His Garden

Ivy. Some roses still bobbing
from the driveway wall. Sick dizzy love
for rotting petals that scab off
in my hands, while the catty voice
needles me. *Love, can you be ever
satisfied? Whose?* Not yet.

And must we always taste your vengeance?
I dig with my fingers. I grease
with spit a thousand mica scratches
and drown the words grubs mutter.
Take it and read. What? Read some song.
I'd eat dirt first to eat my God.

So, the wreckage. Crushed irises,
bitter almonds rattling free,
and blood-burst pomegranate seeds.
All because I was (*Take it, read it*)
obeying, changing my way, for love.
My whole garden became the book.

The Hotel Room Mirror

"But who was it, then, that made her so unhappy?"

A half-room, foreshortened even more
in the huge speckled armoire glass,
the distance chopped, uncrossable,
between your image and where I stood

twiddling the doorknob before I knew
my own key didn't fit, late night,
your interior so underlit
that bluer shadows oozed your forms.

Already still too late, the door
breezed open where your back and thighs
twisted in the green-winged chair,
your body's light coiled, at rest.

Dressed, angled deeper in the surface,
your man pleaded, hands wide, as he flexed
sharp from the bed's protesting edge,
the sheets pinwheeled beneath his weight.

Your glance and his (haphazard,
stark and unconcerned) found mine
in the frame, waiting, though I stayed
invisible to myself, my stare

like your bold forms inhabiting
our depth of field, in the scuffed glass
transcribed. It was already still
too late to save you or be saved.

The Hermit Thrush

Daytime streamed behind the tree line.
Yellow to ghost-green, then something bluer
burnt by darkness. What charmed us
hurt us—the song's crude, remote,
glassy completeness, inside the spruces,
poured a ring around the one
our small talk made. It came again,
a laddered trill, something we felt
in each other's nerves, peaked, then gone.
Another time: behind the trees
(unheard now, unseen) ran the stream
that broke around your sunburnt ankle
and gashed V's in the water glare.
You lifted a foot, chopped your heel
into the current, its axfall *tunk*
absorbed by the stream's oblivion.

And before that (our images
fogged by hours past, passing)
you grabbed and shook my arm, pointing,
sucking breath in a stuttered quiet
soon to cry back as freakish need:
the osprey that for days had pitched
above the river, stooped, cracked
the river's louder rush once,
twice, oaring up through the sky.
A silver thing flapped in its claws.
In our clearing, the hermit's flight
slit the wall of big spruces,
bluer now, night coming down,
needles stacked and cross-stitched black
on black, ripped, sealed tight again,
a place where something song had been.

An Unwritten Letter
to My Daughter

Try to follow me. I think the end will come like this,
in our small town park, around 6 A.M.,

because I imagine light and shade both
rolled to steely, fresh-licked pavings.

Mule deer, down from the hills, thread the cracked wall
of cypress, spade ears twitching at our sound.

It's too early, for them or us, to be here.
The switchback wind grabs the trees, heats them

into Van Gogh's cypresses, orisons, ragged flames
of the mind's uproaring design, alarmed by storm.

Treading timid through the raked trees, the deer charge,
slight skulls ludicrous in rage, then veer away.

The drivenness in trees, lovemaking, any first embarrassed
encounter, the angry jubilance felt along the blood

the first time another's like shape presses into yours
until you feel you've been borrowed by that new form,

O the trees fatten on it. And wind sharpens. This the best
of nature? The big-haunched deer, in dainty retreat

across the tall grass, shrink to bent black squibs,
beautiful crows notched over the world's last wheatfield,

returning to us, restored. The painter was right
to feel such massive calm afterwards. In a final letter

(the field pitches, leaps, sea-infused, unexpectant, whole)
he talked of things "healthful and strengthening, like country sun."

But now the morning's everywhere too much. Drenches shadows,
undefines hedges, smears channelings and coursings,

spills into sewer traps. The sun crosses too far south,
then west, and the jellied ash stuck to chilled air

mocks every childhood memory of favorite windows swabbed
with balm of dust and rain. The world's fine blood

is gone now, the streaming subtext that pulsed unfelt
but sure through all fibers and relations. We're absorbed

by lack in our new life, kindly bloodless shades who stand
speechless in my dreams, politic, ineffectual, and polite.

The snarling packs of dogs leaking from the wood
snap at slow knots of snakes that have found new shade

behind tires of parked cars, then follow the deer spoor
as we must do. There's less time now for poetry's lie

about ecstasy of absence. What does not ever change?
I'm not writing this while there are so many suns.

In Calabria

The fish-bone husband, aslant
behind her paddling hands, checked our plates
then nosed back toward the kitchen.
She stood watching with us;
just beyond the terrace rail
bare-chested men hooted their sons
from the cabin boat listing on chocks
that gouged a crooked trench
toward the small, noiseless surf.

Still Greeks, she said. Sea salt
in their blood, gills and seaweed
for brains sometimes. Boys love it.
We tried once to open a place
back home. Wrong home. Landlocked,
half-dunce for the weird language,
my husband had to bring us back.
Reverend Paisley used to stop
and take a bowl of soup. A bad man then,

a bad man now, visiting his mum.
The plump hands wagged her words
the way she shooed the boat, and boys,
from our terrace, down toward the sea.
Now that's all past. Now is now.
The men peg down the boat, loop ropes
on their shoulders, and walk away,
shouting at the skinny boys
to get back, be good, come on home.

You get such a lousy share
once the broker takes his cut—
a young family, two houses down,
brought swordfish straight to market.
The bonfire, the black-smoke
gasoline stench their boats made,
was like Ulster, like cars. Scorch marks
chip the water while she speaks.
The seabound dark thins out.

A few formica tables, ten customers,
her husband checking plates. Her arms
sweep the terrace: So after Ireland
we took this; it's still too small.
But when we're ready to expand,
the landlord, a nice man, tells us
someone won't be happy. The world
belongs to always someone else.
The full moon breaks the sea.

Above invisible boats, farther out,
fuzzed lanterns dangle, while the reaper
rows a wide quiet circle.
On nights like this, she says,
the anchovies swim toward light
if it's quiet. It's their turn,
because the great one, the swordfish,
can't be caught, so they say,
because the moon's not right.

All Saints

(Halloween: Burlington, Vermont)

— *for Brett*

Should you even remember this?
The sooty red that fell on us;
October's fizzling lakeside light

shimmered off the mud-sun brickface,
once a seed or dry goods store,
the high wall blazing over brash

new economies: bistros,
meditation spas and soap shops;
"Old World" toys like snakewood train sets.

The green King skated past us—
lacquered ducktail, rhinestone jumpsuit,
jolly, martial, fiercer

than the other rolling happy ghouls.
He held hands with the President.
Small old glories yapped at their heels.

All saints, all souls, pumpkin heads
warped in shopwindows, we want back
the longer days we lost last week.

Some endless, deep-freeze winter thrives
where memory was. Each year we see it
clearer, deeper in the ice.

Wanting nothing from my wall,
you spun, pointing (a weather vane)
at the steeple where Church Street ends.

The silvery air exalted it,
and picked at the smart 1816
hatch marks blurred by our distance.

Tenacity, you said, ungrand,
otherworldly, New Englandly.
Just as the black clockface struck five,

a high-wire hum elected us,
summed with our dear monstrosities
in separately imagined half-light.

The Sicilian Vespers

(Teatro Comunale, Bologna, 1986)

A batwing shadow stroked the boxes.
The final act, and wedding bells
toll love's bridal part in slaughter.
Orange groves, blue sky. The peasants
erupt and kill the well-fed French.
("The heart's cry, yes!") They kill some more,
whoever's there. ("Vengeance! Vengeance!")
The white baton flapped from the pit.
We swayed to its call. The pensioners,
old trade unionists, wept and cheered.
Provincial Verdi, fainting in his room,
hears from the straw-decked streets below
the muffled hoofbeats, a village band,
its oom-pa brass and drum, love's mallet
beating time to blood. We fluttered
the exits, in one another's arms.

The New Year's air gagged us. Outside,
we gossiped through the sleet, scarves mashed
to our lips. The gypsies grabbed at us.
Luscious fake orange trees. Scythes, picks.
Nineteen-hundred. The high room's deathbed.

Graffiti, chalky blue-gray spooks,
bled down the theater's orange walls.
The lovers' finest task, they think,
is to outsing each other's grief.
Viva la guerra, viva l'amore.
The gypsies wanted more from us.
Their hungry shadows tossed with ours
against the walls. Artisans, thieves,
shopkeepers, and street people trashed
the governor's palace that stood right here.
They picked it clean. Its timbers and stone

still brace houses all over town.
In '68, on opening night,
students pelted the black-tie crowd.
Unreal love and death contraptions,
overpriced nostalgia, stage tricks
in place of brute cheap history.
We die, or kill, or let be killed,
then wake to other minor terror,
to our intensest selves—angels,
blood and guts, facts, images.
Nearby, six years ago, sweethearts,
summer help, sons, whoever,
traveling second class, were killed
by satchel bombs in a waiting room.
Which of them caught a smell of oranges?
Or saw real bats flying from distant lofts?

Gethsemane

He had nerve enough to follow,
dogging His heels, for what? To learn
a new vocabulary, a prayer,
down there in yellow iris that smelled
like carcass? He came back smiling.
The dog had its day, rolling in meat.
The meat was news: the Word of God
wants what we want, to be unchosen.

He must have made up his mind then.
What if he said, I don't see Him here,
we'll check later? Instead he gagged
on words, like a mouthful of water
brought from the garden, that blood squirms
from the blossom loads and cracked boughs,
and in the stagnant lake of the heart
the sprouting trunk splits, groans,
spilling wine, the spongy dirt
inhaling any blood that falls,
and I'm falling into the tree
and dogs at lakeside bark at clouds . . .

Like that. As if his own speech could
infuriate time while he waited
for an act to come upon him
(as joy sometimes happens). The soldiers
(were they his joy?) got impatient.
So finally his bloodless lips
screamed More life! More salt!
before he gave away his kiss.

Poem

A few bedroom lights.
The moon in windless apple trees
shines across the rooftops,
picking apart hills, empty streets . . .
You're above it all,
sleeping in your room.
No night-sweats or pulsing throat,
no shiver when world-stuff sags,
estranged, unfelt, yet smothers anyway
if love fails in us.
You'll sleep off today's
alcohol flush, the shadow-twitch
of too much dancing,
dreaming back to implausible grins
pimply boys hung on you
before you dumped them in the pit
of your voluptuous indifference. You're watching yourself
smile in that dream. I'm down here, shrill as always,
counting off days in my green time.
Our bachelor locksmith in the corner house
sings through his boozy haze.
He's always alone.

Does anything leave a trace?
I push words around in dirt
tomorrow's rain ploughs under.
Holiday, workday. Wool mills clatter
Goethe's "inhuman noise." Jackboots
plough down Rome's gaunt armies.
Achilles howls at blood he needs to taste.
Behind a shutter on our quiet street,
Augustine sobs into his books.
Our silence is their unforgiving gift.
When I was young, full of myself
and not lost enough to love,
unnerved before some holiday's
solemn terminal bliss,
I buried my head in a pillow.
Late that night, someone else's song
turning and fading around a corner
called me, and calls me now,
caught long gone in my throat.

(After Giacomo Leopardi's *La sera del dì di festa*)

Near Damascus

The antlered scarab rolled a dung ball
for its brood; a red ant, tipsy,
bulldozed a flinty wedge of chaff.
Mud slots caused by recent rain,
now crusted over by the heat—
moon mountains seen close up; my mouth
plugged with road grit and surprise
just when I tried to shout *no*
to the blunt lightning spike that stopped me . . .

In the mountains of the moon I saw
a wasp dragging a grasshopper
to a frothing nest, grubs lingering
through their episode, and larvae
I'd have chewed like honeycomb
if it would have saved my sight.
Antaeus inhaled force from dirt;
he was luckier, never much
for visions, and too far gone.

In my head, I see this body
dumped flat. Painted in above,
the horse twists and straddles me,
his eyes flare, ecstatic, new,
contemptuous of the thing that fell,
while the light shaft curries his flank
and nails me down, the unloved me,
rousted, found out, blasted, saved
down in the road's pearly filth.

Dreaming the Pacific

Then the highway, silver crushed to gray
like poplar bark, glowing as I speed along,
like poplar bark higher where light strikes.

So the light, the coastal sheen, originates
south of me at night, the ocean's exhalation.
My wheels grind on the sound of waves, surf

before flood, for when the water shifts
it's like a night wind flooding poplar boughs:
no sea-foam, no wrack or tidal heave,

but sea-swell risenness. The highway's gone.
My car's running straight upon those grooves
that open every instant before my festive dread

until I feel the earth, now sheeted water
inviolable and calm, pried loose under me,
world's old excess groaning heavenward.

That's when I scream at the flood to carve
its ignorance into an image of my wish,
a topiary stillness of bird or breaking wave.

Old Gold

Maytime pepper plants and geraniums
on scabby balconies. Socks and panties
clocking the breeze. Everything's open.
A hurt peal breaks from a T.V.
and sails down curbside . . .

Then Indian summer: love's betrayal,
earnest, off-key, choking from one
high window. Someone else's trouble,
another season. I go walking
to want just that, at all hours, faulted

and shaky in the narrow streets
of my foreign city. It's no way home.
Once I heard a nest, up there,
crackle with five voices at once
and catch fire.

The streets tonight are empty,
windows shut against snow
no one expected. It falls
like a blessing we can breathe,
as if it were what heaven lost.

My foot ploughs the new form,
skids on the flagstone ground
just enough to pitch me
toward the place I sense
I'd need to fall, to be safe.

A car hums past,
driver and his girl smoldering
in the dash lights. A street sweeper
scythes her broom across the snow,
snagging wrappers and dog turds.

The gypsy rosebud girl
always pauses inside the tavern door,
to catch secrets or guess
who won't buy. We pause, too,
looking up from our food.

The African with her tonight
whooped for *the big boss, the boss man,*
stomping, rattling his velvet shield
of watches, key chains, gold leaf
Eiffel Tower lighters.

A waiter grabbed his elbow
and smiled him back outside.
He's the one I've seen,
or think I saw, moments ago
lashed by headlights. They flayed

a reckless smile from his trapped,
servile fearlessness
where he squatted and picked the sun's
shattered barrettes and money clips
half-sunken in the snow.

The Caverns

Up on the catwalk, icy voices
pinged across the dome's thin air,
our feet rasped against the grid,
and still I felt the long silence
while the sounding stone fell and fell
through the vault's sunless firmament.
They'd entered through the rock eyelet,
then picked their way into the dark,
sizing up the cavern's space,
the sweating minarets, the spires
ridged with gem points, spooled pulpits,
the casual orders resolved, resolving
still, out of millions of years
dripped in water, salt, and rock.

Stooping past the dragonfly wing
that deflected our way, I felt
the stone dropped by the first man in.
A sleet pebble, or fire tooth,
that seared my neck. I jerked back,
and noticed by the snow-lake, minced
with pellets raining from the vault,

one penitent, kneeling in prayer
to the stony whited rain, host
of its own changing form. In time,
the worshiper would be unmade,
transfigured by the melting rock
into cupola, queen, sphinx, or priest,
form's adoration of desire.

I saw that white image again,
incarnate, at the Basilica,
where the sick and lame, pushed along
in draped gurneys and old wheeled chairs,
squared off outside for midday Mass.
Inside, another was being sung.
Incense raveled up the dome's
sun-gashed ribs. Some worshipers
entered Mary's house, kneeling,
or fondled its marble carapace.
Some, with rosaries, stood apart.
Remote, puff-eyed children, staring
every wild way, rocked
and slouched among disheveled pews.

Near, unwatched by them, a man
old enough to be shamed by loss
or want, knelt in a corner,
weeping to his young confessor
whose face, passionate in reply,
imaged political conviction,
the ideologue's righteous love
unchanging. His look assumed a world.

All around, in other boxes,
the wronged, the sorry, the charged will
despairing momentarily
in penitential disarray
waited, astonished, all of us,
by brute divinity in the air.

The want of faith crushed my breath.
Wanting that piece of nature back,
I looked up toward the smoldering dome
and wondered how long it would take
the stone, dropped twenty years ago,
to hit bottom, to be at rest.
The hot finger stung my flesh.
One of the mongol children, puffed face
nodding, grinned at my surprise—
his smile mocked no images,
gave proof of chaotic election,
that touch (his keeper grabbed him, begged
forgiveness) the last ruined gift
that explodes and brings the god.

The Original Rhinestone
Cowboy

is saying, moments after the rainstorm, that he can ignite
ruby and sapphire scales, gemstone chips of every kind,
by picking his guitar, filling his fist with notes,
then tossing a wedding arcade over all our heads:
I'm dreaming jewels for you people. Here they go!
His knobby hands conduct the burger stand's neon buzz,
the day's last light, green and violet sparks (Take them!)
fluttering down last-ditch yellow, delta red marbled
under our car wheels, in oil-slick backwater
we can see offshore. He tells this dream with fact.
He is the original only one. Accept no imitations.
He is homeless, plain unhoused, but glad to be.
His benediction, falling on us who pause to hear,
tips our ears and lashes, returns us to the Garden,
our idea of it at least; we can already taste
the finite shudderings of what was left to us.

His guitar, he says, is a democracy of good intent,
and if some nights it's not so good, that's alright too.
Cars swing into the lot, nick bags from the pickup window

and slide away. The headlights prick tintype sequins
dripping from his buckskin. He gestures down the strip,
to Frostee, U-Haul, fried chicken, crystal used-car domes:
I want you all to dream of being commonwealth,
united in a rhinestone resurrection, proud,
for we're all Americans and have worse things in store.
Trucks grinding toward the interstate toot twice for luck.
He waves: I'm someone who's not going someplace else,
I'm an original, I don't travel too well.
To the rain-smeared cars, the strip, the truckers, to us,
he confers the rest of nothing's colors in his hands:
Bless you children. Fear not the rain. I say
bless you all. The O.R.C. says just you wait.

Three Poems

1.

(*for M.J.*)

More conclusions. Moonlight, moonshine,
another year done, under a blue moon.
Eve's puffed, eyeless face pleads
for unconsciousness. Adam's already
a mineral stalk with sex and legs.
We want to remember everything,
track senseless piecemeal moments
into keen incoherence. That's our trouble.
Who needs to remember anything?
We catch sight of ourselves at night
stumbling into a bush, my shade
squalling across yours. My birthday month,
December's lunar completeness—
we remember when we were young,
still unknown to ourselves, unfinished
now more than ever. In our happiest moments
we think it's wisdom to call back
any pain that freezes us in place.

2.

Heartsick, settled for good,
you think you finally know something . . .
You had what seemed to last,
one more last false thing.
You drank hope for its thrill,
but believed in it. Now belief
burns off with the thrill.
You could live with, even love,
the way things seemed.
Words were all part of the plot.
You worked. Is anything really worth
the will and rage and trouble?
Life galls and bleeds us dry.
What's left? The world, our slime.
So, give it up one last time.
The species ends in each of us.
Nature, brute force, malingering,
outlives us and makes the world
a common grave and everything
an inexpressible emptiness.

3.

It now feels like a world beyond:
all this, my favorite hill, the hedge
blocking the horizon's better part . . .
My mind roughs out the rest, farther,
where space doesn't stop, and silence
expands like harmless numb dream time.
My heart catches at the thought.
The vacant plenty I imagine
runs with the wind storming these trees;
then I invite eternity, the lost seasons,
my own moment's noise. I exist
to crack the perfect image,
the thing I love, then lose it
in the sumptuous chaos of my heart.

(After Giacomo Leopardi's *Alla luna, A se stesso,
L'infinito*)

After the Sacrifice

Abraham

Nothing turned his head. Not the whining rigs
hauling timber on the interstate below,
not even the hummingbird's green wings
thrumming past our ears. Toneless. Banal.
No imagination adorned or enthralled the act
already in his head like a common dream.
He had his ram's dullard glum face,
hilariously intent, serious beyond belief,
a deliberateness clarified to superb indifference.
Like the look sometimes on the faces of sowers,
or assembly line workers, who learn dullness
by need, not rule, unexpectant, focused,
exact, crass even. Climbing the slope,
a light breeze switching through the evergreens,
he rolled his haunches, bolting down each footstep
like the ram we all trailed. I felt
the only words he thought: Do what you're told.
What I was doing. But he had all that blood,
and bone-rattling conscience. He seemed glad for once

to be no middle ground, no half-delivered alien
flesh to a world law taught him not to cling to.
Given something to do, he mugged, justified and pure.
He could have been tossing seeds on fiddleheads
drowsing under the trees, or changing work stations
in a sluggish dream. To be a man of unwilled destiny.
He wouldn't ask what power made that his desire.
Unlike the other, who had much less to do.

The Other One

walked with a baboon's teenage swagger: ropy arms,
the hard tulip trunk wielding such forgetful force
he could have snapped the old man's neck. He lived
in the world's blood, ram's blood, household order
sustained by sacrifice. I felt the language in his head,
pinwheeled stops and starts, carnival vanes blown
by colors trapped in tall trees, the stream and glacial rock,
streaked shadows dripping from the pines, field mice,
tires, deer nibbling bark, the soft tear of flesh
now in a raptor's beak, the ram held to the rock,
the skinning knife suddenly at his ear, a father
pinning him, reeking of damp wool, blood bits, salt . . .
Perfect strangers, they couldn't believe each other's life.
And mum—all the noise was in their heads. Until the boy
looked back, his crooner's mouth gnawing the air
to say, as if he just remembered, *Again?*

Frankie's Birthday Party

Atlantic City's littlest bedouin, he says,
and his wife turns toward him, as if she knows
where it's bound to end. I was, I swear to God,
the littlest transfixed Arab, bandaged in towels
so that the sand wouldn't contaminate my skin,
and all those greased thighs and arms around me
made it worse: grown-ups looked as if they squirmed
wet from some fat mother. On the boardwalk,
I shook hands with Mr. Peanut; remember, honey,
my telling you that, too? The Steel Pier's Diving Horse
kaboomed the water tank. The taffy machine
cranked sexy pink cables—*it* could eat *you,*
I swear, and give you nightmares of jelly pillows
grabbing like rubber breakers or flesh.

"He wakes up," she tells us, smiling entirely at him,
"grunting, and like he's pushing back invisible walls:
Get these fucking things away, give me air somebody!"
I see that child of myself, he says,
and know he never died, and yet I want him
as if he belonged to someone else. I've seen those kids
on Ninth Street, bagging tomatoes, hauling apple crates;

their muscles twitch like horseflesh. Ten years I'm gone,
and they're still competing, trading epithets
like Homer's princes, or almost like: one guy yells
to the general crowd, *Your Siamese pigskin mother!*
Another, three stalls down, shouts back: *Your Mongolian
Pekinese Plasticine mother!*
                                             "And now,
can you believe it? Philadelphia's only bedouin
becomes, at an advanced age, a humdinger historian."
But she's the only one not from our place.
She says that as if to cool the story of return.
We could get lost. French fries in paper cones,
grease slicking our fingers like suntan oil;
blinking Pokerino screens, The Wild Mouse, quoits;
and back home, the glittering peacock fan
from fireplugs in August, bottlecaps and deathbox
on tacky streets. Now—the voice quickens—
my mother grabs the gambler's shuttle on weekends
to blow her pension on the slots. She'll never learn.

The cake, after pizza, tastes so sweet and sluggish
we breathe through our mouths and cool the thirst
with more beer. He smiled through the song, his wife
holding his hand between both of hers,
but he's not eating, hasn't been. When he picks up,
it sounds like more of the same, his voice clear,
becalmed, the air still combed with candle smoke,
that in the other time he won't forget,
no more than he'd forget the sand and taffy, it was fun
to be last man out and torch a village.
Not to watch it, but to do it, leave it,
then you never wanted to see it again. You lost it.
That part, too, comes back, not the sickening fear,
but the knowledge that fun is what it truly was.